In Time for Church

EILEEN DISTASIO-CLARK

Copyright © 2024
All Rights Reserved

With Great Love and Appreciation to Those Who Have and Do Bless My Life.

My Family:

Joseph DeStasio Sr. & Miriam Lucille Baragone DeStasio, My Late Parents.

Andrea Jean DeStasio McIntosh, My Older Sister and Their Families.

Joseph DeStasio Jr., My Younger and Only Brother and Their Families.

Donna Marie DeStasio Wagner, My Younger Sister and Their Families.

My Children:

Eileen, Rebekah, Rachel, S. Michael, Jennifer, Sharon, Tara, Stephanie, Apryll, Mikaelah, & M. Trevor and THEIR Families!!

ACKNOWLEDGEMENTS

First and foremost, I express, deeply, my sincere gratitude to our Heavenly Father for blessing me with the gift and talent of writing! I know I could not do what I do without His assistance.

I also want to acknowledge and express gratitude to the members of my birth family—Joseph Sr., Miriam, Andrea, Joseph Junior, and Donna. All the experiences of my childhood years, experiences that taught me so very much and enabled me to reveal my true self to myself, came about through my experiences and relationships with them.

And, of course, it goes without saying, but I will say it anyway: I also want to acknowledge and note my gratitude to my children, Eileen, Rebekah, Rachel, S. Michael, Jennifer, Sharon, Tara, Stephanie, Apryll, Mikaelah, and M. Trevor, and their families! Through multiple things they said to me, over multiple years, I finally came to the realization that

Heavenly Father gave me the gift of writing and opened the doors to these experiences because He knew that by sharing them with others, others could feel His love too.

And He definitely wants us all to know that He, Heavenly Father, Heavenly Mother, and Jehovah truly do loves us!!!

INTRODUCTION

There are sixteen books in this series, which I refer to as *"The Ellie Series."* All of the characters in these stories portray real people from my life. The main characters depict the members of my family: Daddy is my daddy; Mommy is my mommy; Jeannie is my older sister; Junior is my brother; Maria is my younger sister, and Ellie is me. Now, those are not our actual first names, but they do reference us.

The first story in the series presents our Heavenly Father's Plan of Salvation and takes place in the Pre-Earth World. Now, of course, because we all—when we were born—received what is known as The Veil of Forgetfulness, I do not actually remember everything from or about the Pre-Earth World, but I do know about and understand it from much study and worship as a member of The Church of Jesus Christ of Latter-Day Saints, and memories restored to me through the Holy Spirit. So, from this story there is much truth to be learned.

The last story in the series is set in the Post-Mortal World, and presents a depiction of what happens to us after this life. Again, because I have not gone there yet, I cannot say I 'remember' this.

But, I have also learned about the Post-Mortal World from much study and worship as a member of The Church of Jesus Christ of Latter-Day Saints.

All of the other stories are based on true events from my life; events that actually occurred when and how they are depicted in these stories. I chose these events because they are among the many occurrences in my life that presented—or revealed that which I already knew without having to be taught—Principles of Eternal Truths.

Also, I chose these events as the settings for my stories because they depict wonderful learning moments from my childhood and adolescent years, lessons that have blessed and benefited me throughout the whole of my life and will forever continue to do so. Also, through these great truths and their consequences in my life, I have been able to share them with many others, whose lives have also been blessed by them.

So, please, read and enjoy, then care and share the messages and stories with others!!

Now, there are also a couple of things you can look for:

In each story, the title of the previous story is presented in *italicized* form, the title of the next story is presented in *Capitalized Italicized* form, and the title of the story being read is presented in **emboldened** form.

Also, every story has at least one word that is uncommon or 'created.'

So, as you read, search, find, and have fun!

IN TIME FOR CHURCH

"You cannot stand in the middle, Veste; there is no middle," Orsea explained, as they walked along the Path of Progression toward the Pavilion of Perfection. "We have to choose; we either go with Father's Plan, or we do not. But if we do not, we will lose the opportunity to have everything we said we want, to become like our Parents and be able to do the things They do, and have Eternal Families."

"How do you know that?" Veste asked with a hint of irritation.

"I have learned, Veste," Orsea replied, with a touch of annoyance, but with a heap of concern, "and so have you. We have had many discussions in our council meetings about The Plan of Salvation. Father and Mother have taught us well. They have explained everything we need to know and do to become like Them. They even shared the experiences They had in the mortal world in which They proved Themselves and by which They became exalted. And, They did not stop there. They told us about some of Their brothers and sisters who made different choices, choices that limited their progression."

As they approached the pavilion, Orsea stepped in front of Veste, and with loving intentions, in an attempt to further answer his question, she posed to him a few questions of her own.

"I was always at our council meetings, so that I could learn all that was being taught, all that Father and Mother were teaching us; were you?

"I listened intently and contemplated deeply all that They presented to us, all that They discussed with us; did you?

"I talked with Them, after those meetings, and pondered seriously that which They shared with us; did you?

"I know that what we have been told and shown is Eternal Truth, and Veste, we cannot change that. Do you know that? Do you believe that?"

"Please," Orsea pleaded, as she took Veste's hand and then turned to face him as she stepped up onto the pavilion, "understand this, Veste; because our Parents have endowed us with agency—the right and the ability to make our own choices—we can choose to accept or reject the truth, believe or deny the truth, live or defy the truth, but we cannot change the truth. And ultimately, when we have completed our mortal probation, all of us, whether we choose to accept or reject it, believe or deny it, live or defy it, will be judged by it—by that truth that we have been taught, and have accepted."

"So, we just have to do what They say?" Veste asked, in a mildly frustrated tone.

"No," Orsea responded gently, but resolutely, and with a hint of impatience, "that is not a correct understanding, Veste, and you know that it is not. If you do not want to do what They did, you do not have to. If you do not want to choose as They chose, you do not have to. If you do not want to live your life according to The Plan They designed for us—designed for our benefit—you... do... not... have... to... But Veste, if you do not, then you cannot expect to have what They have, or to be as They are."

As Veste and Orsea sat down at the head of the pavilion, with a small group of brothers and sisters gathering around them, Veste began to counter with, "But Lucifer said—"

"Forget what Lucifer said!" Orsea interjected firmly and with emphatic emotion. "He knows, and he knew even before he started the trouble that led to the war, that there is only one way for us to be able to become like our Parents. If we are to gain all that They have gained, and become able to continue our Eternal Progression as They have, we must make our own choices to do what is right, and that means right according to the Eternal Laws that we have been taught.

"Lucifer wanted to force us to do as he directed, not because he cared about us, but because he wanted all of the credit for everyone's progression—

all of our Parent's glory. But, if we had sided with him and let him, or anyone else, make those choices for us, or force us to make those choices, right as they might have been, we would still not have been able to gain Exaltation and become as our Parents are."

"Why? Why would that not be enough?" Veste questioned with confused frustration. "If the choice is right, it is right."

"Yes," Orsea replied, again with loving concern, but also with steadfast assurance, "you are right; what is right, is right. But, if you are not the one making that right choice, if you are just doing what you are told to do, how could you possibly learn anything? How would you even know that what you are doing is really right, or why it is right?"

"Lucifer would have told me," Veste replied.

"Would you have believed him?" Orsea asked, astounded by his response. Then with the intention of encouraging deeper thought on Veste's part, she asked, "How could you know that what he would tell you would really be right?"

To demonstrate her point, Orsea pointed to Hyahn, a young brother who had sat down next to her, and said, "We all know that Hyahn is very good at creating novae, and I do not doubt that he would be happy to make one for you, Veste."

Then, directing her words to Hyahn, Orsea asked, "Right?"

Hyahn, sounding like he was almost offended by the question, replied with obvious emotional emphasis, "Yes! Of course, I would!"

Orsea smiled broadly at Hyahn, then turned back to Veste and continued with, "But, if Father gave you an assignment to make a nova, and it was Hyahn creating that nova for you, just so you could say that it was done, it would be done, but you would not know how to do it, because you would not have done it. Right?"

"Well... yeah," Veste agreed reluctantly.

"Well, Veste," Orsea continued, "the same principle applies to the making of our own choices in the temporal mortal world. If we do not make our own choices, we cannot progress, because we will not have learned anything that we do not already know, and that is not enough for us to become more than what we already are.

"Look, I am telling you, and it was Father and Mother who told all of us, that just as we have made our own choices here, in TreLampor, in order to earn the privilege and gain the ability to enter Areth, the temporal world that was created for our mortal experience, we need to be the ones making our own choices there, so that we will be worthy and able to return to our Heavenly Home, exalted and glorified.

"They know this is true because They did it. They experienced the effects of choices made in a mortal world. I have accepted Their testimonies and I am sharing them with you because I know they are true. But do you believe me? Do you know, I mean really know, that what you have been told is right, just because I have told you?" Orsea asked.

"I... I... I guess so," was Veste's uncertain, and somewhat irritated reply.

To which, Orsea, already knowing the answer, but to point out the point she was working on making, asked, "But you do not really know; do you?"

Veste was silent. He did not know how to answer Orsea's question because he knew he could not challenge it. So, she continued, "Veste, the reason we need to make our own choices is because that is the only way we will learn what we need to learn in order to become what we need to become, so as to be able to obtain all that we have said we—all that we have chosen to have—all that we have elected to become!"

Then, more fully aware of the group that had gathered, and always jumping on an opportunity to teach, Orsea directed her words to include everyone,

"Do you all not recall what Father explained to us in the last Council Meeting? He made it very clear, that if we want to be like Them—our Parents—and be able to do all that They do, and live with Them for all Eternity, we must...," Orsea paused and thought for a moment, then continued with, "go to school. Yes! That is what I will call it... school, and while we are there, we will have to face hardships.

"Those hardships will be... hmmmm..." Orsea thought for another moment, then continued with, "Our coursework. Yes! That is what they will be: coursework. And as course work, while they will be difficult in many ways and, at times, the cause of uncomfortable sorrows, they will be the means through which we will learn what is right and why it is right, and through which we will be able to grow and enhance our knowledge and abilities."

"So, are you saying life in the mortal world will be terrible?" Veste asked, with obvious irritation.

"No, I am not!" Orsea answered, matter-of-factly. "Yes, there will be trials, challenges, and sufferings, but there will also be many good times and many blessings. In all that we experience, good or bad, we will have to choose how we will respond. Those moments will be our tests, and the choices we make will determine the grades we get and what degree we receive."

In response to a tug on her hand, Orsea looked at Iterah, the little sister sitting in front of her. Then, with a sweet, quiet expression of longing for understanding, Iterah asked, "Degree? What is that?"

Orsea smiled, held Iterah's hand in hers, and said, "Let me explain that, like this. Think back for a moment, to when Lucifer and his followers were still here in TreLampor. You do remember how Lucifer wanted to modify the Plan for our Salvation that Father and Mother offered to us; right?"

"Yes," Iterah replied, then added, "but I do not know if I know why."

"Well," Orsea said, and then explained, "I guess we can say that he wanted to be the boss, the only one to make the choices that needed to be made. He wanted to take away from us the freedom to choose, and just tell us what to do. When his plan was rejected, and of course, we know it could not have worked, he began a war. Do you know why?"

"I can answer that," replied Anjodo, the brother sitting next to Iterah. With confidence, typical of his nature, he explained, "He was mad because Father did not let him have his way. So, he tried to get everyone to follow him, probably thinking he could change Father's mind, if enough of us went along with him."

"Yes, Anjodo, you are right," Orsea said, "then what happened?"

"Well," Anjodo continued, "Lucifer, and everyone who followed him, caused so much trouble trying to convince all of us to agree with them, that Father said they could not live here anymore."

"Yes," Orsea confirmed, "they were cast out of TreLampor, but not just because they wanted to do things differently. Through their opposition to Father's Plan and their aggressiveness against all who did not accept their way, they halted their own ability to progress and thereby became unworthy and unable to have a physical body and to become perfected and glorified like our Parents. That is why they were expelled, becoming… hmmmm…" Orsea again pondered for a little moment, then concluded, "We can call them Heavenly Drop-Outs."

Everyone smiled and some chuckles were heard, as Orsea continued, "Now, it is important to understand that if, either here in TreLampor, or on Areth, any of us were to choose to do what they did and turn away from Father and against His Plan, we would suffer the same fate that they are, and always will be suffering. We would become, as they did,

Heavenly Drop-Outs, with no opportunity to ever come home. We would, as they will, live forever, as Sons and Daughters of Perdition, in Outer Darkness, a cold, lonely, bleak, miserable place, where there is no light, no family connection, and no further progression.

"We cannot even image what that must be like because we have never known anything like it. We only know about it. Still, we know enough to know that it is not a desirable place, but that is what we would be choosing as our Eternal Destiny, if we were to choose to do as Lucifer and his followers did.

"Try to think about that, what it would be like to feel lonely, miserable, deeply depressed, angry, and who knows how else—all bad feelings, not good ones—forever and ever and ever and... well, you get the idea. It most definitely is not a condition that would or could, in any way, be desirable.

"It is Father's Plan that will bring us all the love, joy, happiness, growth, progression, and more—all that there is to have—all that we said we wanted. Consider that carefully. Do not let yourself forget, not just what you chose, by why you chose it. I think the fate of Lucifer and his followers demonstrates very well the great importance and value of always holding tightly to the Rod of Eternal Truth."

Orsea paused. Looking over the group, studying and contemplating their expressions, she tried to determine whether there was or was not understanding of that which was being discussed. After concluding that there was, she continued with, "Now, it is also important to understand that mere acceptance of Father's Plan does not guarantee that we will receive everything that it offers."

"Why not?" Rojisha, the sister sitting next to Veste, questioned in a bewildered intonation.

"Because," Orsea responded, looking at Rojisha, but directing her words to everyone, "by choosing to follow Father's Plan and fulfilling the ordinances required here, we chose, and became worthy to go to Areth—to school—knowing that we will not remember our Heavenly Home nor all that we have learned here.

"We will be endowed with The Light of Christ so that we will be able to distinguish right from wrong, but we will have to use the power of faith to learn, to choose, to do, and to become more than we already are. After all, if we already knew what we need to go to a temporal mortal world to learn, we would not need to go there; but we do not know, so we do need to go! And, because we have never had such an experience, we will make mistakes."

"Do we have to do that?" Iterah asked, with a touch of sadness in her words.

Again, taking Iterah's hand in hers, and responding tenderly, Orsea explained, "No, Iterah, making mistakes is not a requirement, but it is something that will happen because we will not always know what we are to do. Remember, we will be learning many new things.

"Now, of course, just because we will make mistakes, does not mean that all will be lost to us. We will be able to correct the mistakes we make and be forgiven. That is why Jehovah accepted the calling of Redeemer and became our Atoning Savior; so we can be forgiven.

"Now, we will have to use faith to make the choices we will need to make. How well we choose, how much we learn, the nature of what we do with what we learn, and what we become because of all that we learn will determine which degree we will receive.

"Surely, we all remember what Father and Mother told us about the education that will be available to us in the mortal world. In fact, They even informed us that some of us will be a part of the discoveries that will bring it to light. They also explained that the level of education acquired will be identified through what will be called degrees—Associate Degree, Bachelor Degree, Master Degree, and Doctoral Degree."

"Oh," Veste interjected thoughtfully, "so somewhat like the instruction that we have had here, and the difference between where Lucifer got stuck and where we can go."

"Yes, Veste," Orsea said, "that is right. Now, of course, the schooling we will receive in Areth will be a bit different than that which we received here in TreLampor. A lot of it will be for the purpose of receiving knowledge about the temporal mortal world in which we will be living. But a portion of it will be far more important than that!

"It will be for the purpose of learning what we need to know and becoming what we need to become in order to return Home to our Heavenly Parents, fit to receive all that we have chosen to go there to get. That education will come only in part from formal teaching. Most of it, and the most important parts of it, will come through the experiences that we will live and the choices that we will make.

"Each one of us, when it is our time to go, will be sent to Areth, the place I am calling school. We can think of it as... hmmmm... let us call it, The University of Life."

Iterah smiled at Orsea and said, "I like that."

"Thank you," Orsea replied. Then returning the smile, she continued, "Based upon the choices we make and what we choose to become, we can receive frooommm..."

Orsea smiled as she motioned to Iterah, and Iterah, returning the smile, said with confidence, "The University of Life!"

Orsea nodded, then continued with "The least degree, which we can call an Associate's Degree in Telestial Glory, or a higher degree, which we can call a Bachelor's Degree in Terrestrial Glory, or an even higher degree, which we can call a Master's Degree in Celestial Glory. Or, we can go all the way to the Eternal Top and receive a Doctoral Degree in Exaltation!"

Orsea smiled as everyone chuckled aloud; they always enjoyed the way Orsea explained things. It was amusing, but it also made sense to them. Well, at least to most of them, most of the time, but sometimes a little more explanation was needed, at least for some of them. That was why Rojisha asked, curiously, "What does all of that mean?"

"It is my way of identifying the different kingdoms that Father and Mother taught us about," Orsea replied.

"Oh, yeah," Rojisha said, and then asked, "will you explain those again, please?"

"Sure," Orsea replied, "but first, let me explain what Paradise and Prison are, because they are also a part of the journey between Areth and the Eternal Kingdoms."

Apparently, those who had gathered in the group were interested in knowing more about that journey and those places. That became evident because they moved in closer and became reverently silent as Orsea began her explanation.

"When we leave TreLampor, we will go directly to Areth, where we will receive our physical body and proceed through the experiences that will enable us to grow beyond our present state of progression. However, when we leave Areth, we will not go directly to the Kingdom of Glory; in fact, we will not even truly leave Areth.

"We will first go—in spirit form, without the physical body—either to a Spiritual Paradise or to a Spiritual Prison, worlds that are on Areth, but not in the physical, temporal dimension; rather, they are in a Spirit Dimension. It is there that we will await the Day of Resurrection.

"In that world, just as there has been here in TreLampor and will be on Areth, there will still be tasks to perform, works to do, and much to learn, but not all Spirit Beings will be interacting together. You see, whatever were the attitudes, appetites, and desires—the traits of a person in the temporal state—will be the same traits in the post mortal, spirit state. So, those who were righteous when they were on Areth will still be righteous when they enter the Spirit World, and those who were wicked when they were on Areth will still be wicked when they enter the Spirit World. That is why there are two segments, Paradise and Prison, in the Post Mortal Spirit World.

"Those who were righteous in mortality and received, and then lived according to Father's Law, will go to Paradise, where they will live with great joy, peace, and comfort. Those who were not obedient, who chose to do that which they knew was wrong, those who did not repent of their wrongs, and those who did not have the opportunity to receive Father's Laws in mortality will go to Prison, where they will experience sorrow, suffering, and confinement.

"However, because they will still have the opportunity to choose between good and evil, those who had not learned about Father's Laws, but were good people when they lived on Areth, will still have the opportunity to be taught His Laws, when they are in Prison, by those who are in Paradise. If they accept and live according to those Laws, and repent of all their wrongs, they will be able to leave Spirit Prison and enter Paradise. Those who do not choose to repent or accept Father's Law will remain in Prison.

"It is there, in Paradise or Prison, that all will remain until the Day of Resurrection. On that day of Final Judgement, we will be righteously judged according to our works, words, attitudes, and level of progression and then receive the degree or glory that we have earned.

"Now, we all know that when those who were cast out of TreLampor were cast out of TreLampor, they were actually cast down to Areth, but in spirit form, having lost all opportunity to have a physical body or to gain any glory... ANY glory! That is why I refer to them as Heavenly DropOuts; they never can and never will receive any Degree of Glory.

"Of course, that did not make them happy. So now, because Lucifer and his little devils are lightyears beyond outraged, filled with furiosity, they do not want any of us to have what they no longer can have. That is why they will never stop trying to pull us away from the truth, and why the war Lucifer started here continues there. That is why, when we are living on Areth, experiencing the experiences that will make up the course work of our education there, they will unceasingly work to confuse us, to convince us to make wrong choices, to commit sins, and to turn away from Father's Plan."

"And because life on Areth will be a new experience for us," Anjodo added, "that is why we will make mistakes, and that is why, when Jehovah went to Areth, He did what He did because we needed a Savior and that was what He needed to do to become our Savior. Right?"

"Yes, Anjodo, that is correct," affirmed Orsea. "But just as we will not be forced to make the right choices, we will also not be forced to repent of the wrong ones and of the mistakes we make either. That too, will be our choice to do, or to not do."

"So, by repenting, even though we will still not be perfect, we will be able to get what we want," Hyahn stated thoughtfully but quizzically, "but if we do not repent, we will lose it all; right?"

"Well, yes and no," Orsea replied. "It is more than just a matter of do or do not, it is also a matter of how much we do, how well we do what we do, and why we choose to do what we do. That is why there are different degrees or glories.

"Hard as it may be to believe this, at least for some of us, not everyone will care enough to do all that we must do to gain all that there is to gain. Sadly, but truthfully, many, when they have erred or sinned, will not repent. Either they will not feel sorry for the things they did, or they will blame someone else for their choices and think that clears them of accountability, or they will convince themselves that, as long as they do not do it again, whatever it was, they will be okay, or they just will not care. They may even think they can repent later, but they will find that they are wrong.

"Those who leave Areth without having repented, knowing that they needed to repent, will have to suffer for their own sins when they enter Spirit Prison, and that is where they will go because they will not be worthy to enter Paradise. Now, even then, after they have atoned for their own sins, because they will not have allowed themselves to progress enough to gain anything else, they will only be able to enter the Telestial Kingdom…"

"And," Rojisha added as she smiled at Orsea, "they will receive the Associate's Degree in Telestial Glory. Right?"

"Yes," Orsea said, returning the smile, "that is right." She then continued with, "Because they chose to not repent of the things they did that they knew were wrong, while they were on Areth, they could not progress any farther than that. They could not become worthy or able to endure any greater glory than the Telestial, and because of that, their powers and progression will be severely limited."

"Sooo, does that mean they will be punished forever?" Veste asked.

"No," Orsea replied, "not punished. They will still be receiving a degree of glory, but they will also be suffering what Father identified as Eternal Damnation. You all know, right, what damnation is?"

"Yeah, we probably do," Anjodo responded, "but would you explain it anyway, just in case someone needs more clarification?"

"You mean, just in case you need more clarification?" Rojisha teased.

"Well...," Anjodo said with a mischievous smirk that verified Rojisha's accusation.

"Sure," Orsea said, chuckling a little before proceeding to explain. "Picture this; on Areth there will be oceans, rivers, lakes, streams, creeks, puddles, you know, the bodies of water. When we are there, we will be able to use some of them to fulfill some of our needs.

"One of the ways we will be able to do that is by building a barrier, a structure or a wall, called a dam, to direct and redirect, and control the water's flow. That structure, which, as I said, is called a dam, will stop the natural course of the running waters. Therefore, we can say that the dam, when placed in the path of running waters, creates its damnation. In different words, it stops the water's flow or progression.

"That is what happens to those who sin but, knowingly, choose to not repent. They stop their own progression. They will have advanced enough to enter the Telestial Kingdom, but no more than that. And, because the Veil of Forgetfulness, that will withhold our memory of TreLampor while we are on Areth, will be removed when we leave Areth, they will recall all that they have learned and chosen here, in TreLampor, all that they said they wanted, and all that they did or did not do on Areth that prevented them from receiving it. So, while there will be a measure of happiness and peace for those assigned to the Telestial Kingdom ~ joy far beyond what anyone could ever obtain, or imagine on Areth ~ they will also and forever know the sorrow that will come from the realization that they could have had so very much more, all that they said they wanted, but lost, because of their own choices, because they built their own dam."

"Sooo... what will we have to do to repent?" Veste asked.

"Well, first, we will have to acknowledge that the choice or behavior we chose was wrong," Orsea began to explain.

"And we will know that it is... how?" Veste asked.

"Through the Light of Christ," Hyahn said to Veste, "which is the basic knowledge and understanding of what is right and what is wrong." Then looking at Orsea, he asked, "Right?"

"Yes, Hyahn, that is right," Orsea replied, then added, "We will also have the Holy Spirit to guide us, and we will be taught by our mortal parents and others who will help care for and teach us. We will also learn right from wrong through our experiences."

"That sounds easy enough," Veste said.

"Oh, but that is just the beginning," Orsea said, and then continued with, "along with acknowledging that what we did was wrong, we will have to be genuinely regretful for having done it."

"That kind of true remorse is not going to feel good!" came a soft and gentle voice from the far side of the pavilion. It was Jehovah, who, as He advanced to the front of the group, and sat down next to Orsea, continued to explain, "Along with that, you will have to be humble enough to admit to Father, and to whomever you may have hurt, that you are deeply and sincerely sorry for what you did. That is the water that will begin the cleansing process.

"You will also need to set things right in whatever way you can, and then, you will be able, and required to ask Father to forgive you. Finally, as you work to forsake the sin, the Atonement will provide the soap that will wash you clean."

"And that is why we needed You to do what You did," Rojisha tenderly affirmed.

"Yes," Orsea confirmed, "that is why we all need His sacrifice, and will need His guidance when we are on Areth."

"So then," Veste asked, "is that what will bring us home?"

Orsea looked at Jehovah with a questioning expression. She did not know if she should answer or let Him answer, but He said, "Teach them, Orsea, all that you know."

"Well," Orsea began, "it is part of what we need to do to come home, but it is not everything. Along with repenting when we sin, we must live the best lives that we can live on Areth. We must engage in proper learning, and do all the good that we can do, but if we stop there, even if we have chosen to follow Father's Plan, and repent when needed, we will only be prepared for the Terrestrial Kingdom." Then, directing her words to Rojisha, she asked, "And what degree is that?"

"The Bachelor's Degree in Terrestrial Glory?" Rojisha replied with a hint of uncertainty.

"Yes," Orsea confirmed with a smile and a nod, "that is correct."

"So, are you saying that to live a good life is not good enough?" Veste asked with obvious annoyance.

"I guess I am." Orsea replied, "It is good enough for the good, but not good enough for the best."

"What are you saying?" Veste questioned with irritation.

"Veste," Jehovah, in a quiet, but firm voice of love and correction, said, "you know what she is saying. To live a good life, being kind and caring, repenting of wrongs, and serving others, will bring to you great growth and much learning. You will be worthy and able to obtain Terrestrial Glory, which is a great and marvelous glory. But if you want all that Father and Mother desire for us to have, all that They presented to us, taught to us in our Council Meetings, all that we said we wanted, you must make additional covenants, or promises, and live up to them."

"And, Veste," Orsea interjected, "though the Terrestrial Kingdom will be far greater than the Telestial, I believe those who go there will also experience the same remorse that is born of the knowledge that they could have had more, but, by their own choices, they could only receive less. Though their sorrow will be experienced to a lesser degree, it will, nonetheless, be sorrow and damnation."

"Sorrow," Jehovah emphasized, "because they will, as Orsea explained, remember all there is to remember and know that it was by their own choices that they could not receive what they said they wanted, and damnation because they will not be able to progress any farther than that."

"So, what are those covenants?" Iterah asked with quiet sincerity.

Again, Orsea looked at Jehovah wondering if she should answer, or if He would. Finally, in response to His encouraging expression, she explained, "They are special promises that are a part of the Plan of

Salvation and will aid us in our learning and growth. They will need to be made through proper temple worship, which will be available to those who accept and live the Gospel Law that Jehovah has taught and will teach on Areth.

"Now, some of us will be able to do exactly that while we are living in the temporal world. However, because of the many struggles that have prevailed and will prevail on Areth, not everyone will be able to partake of that blessing while in mortality. That is why Father's Plan makes it possible for those who will not be able to go to the temple when they are there, to receive those covenants through proxy when they are in the Spirit World."

"What does that mean?" Hyahn asked.

"That means this," Orsea said, "someone who has already received the covenants for him or herself can do the temple work for another person, one who has already lived on and left Areth. Then, that person can choose to accept or reject the work that was done. If accepted, it is received by that person, as if it had been done by that person."

"How does that work?" asked Hyahn.

This time Jehovah answered, "The same way the Atonement works. It was I who suffered the pain and sorrow for the wrongs that were and would be committed by all of our Parent's children. Through that sacrifice, and upon the condition of true repentance, the effects of sin are washed away, enabling reconciliation between the truly repentant person and Father and Mother. Proxy works in like manner."

Then looking at Orsea with an expression of tender appreciation, he said, "Orsea will be one of those who does attend Father's temple. She will receive those ordinances for herself. Then, she will go back to the temple and receive the same ordinances again, and again, and again, every time she returns.

"Now, of course, she will not be doing all that work over for herself; that will not be necessary. She will be doing the work for her family and for others who did not have the opportunity to attend a temple when they were on Areth.

"Orsea will speak for them the words of the covenants; she will do for them what needs to be done, but they will be the ones to choose whether that work will be accepted or rejected. If they do accept it, then the outcome of Orsea's work will be transferred to them, in the same manner that the effects of My Atonement are transferred to the repentant sinner. If they do not accept it, then their progression will be halted, regardless of how good they lived their mortal lives, because without those covenants, they can progress no further. In like manner, the effect of My Atonement cannot be transferred to those who do not repent."

"Can anyone do that work for others?" asked Rojisha.

"Anyone who has accepted Father's Law, or the Gospel as it will be called on Areth," Jehovah responded, "and has been to the temple and made those covenants for him or herself, and who remains worthy."

"And," Orsea added, "it is by making or receiving, and honoring those covenants that we will become worthy and able to advance beyond Terrestrial Glory and return to the Celestial Kingdom."

"Where we will receive the Master's Degree in Celestial Glory," Rojisha said with confidence.

"Yes!" Orsea said with a playful tilt of her head and a smile of confirmation.

"So then, if that brings us home, what is the Doctoral Degree for?" Rojisha asked.

"That is the degree of progression that enables us to not just return Home to be in the presence of our Parents, but to become like our Parents," Orsea explained. "We can only obtain that through eternal marriage, the highest covenant made in the temple. Anyone, on his or her own merit alone, as an individual, can enter into any of the other kingdoms, even the lesser degrees of glory in the Celestial Kingdom, to be as the angles.

"But even those in the lower levels of the Celestial Kingdom will suffer a degree, much, much, much smaller though it may be, due to the great, great, great, great glory of the Celestial Kingdom, the same type of remorse and damnation as those in the Telestial and Terrestrial Kingdoms, for they too will remember what they could have had, what they said they wanted, how close they came to getting it, but, by their own choice, could not receive it.

"Now, to become exalted, to enter into the highest degree of Celestial Glory, we must come as a couple, as husband and wife, having repented of all our wrongs, having lived truly good lives in accordance with Father's Laws, having taken upon ourselves the temple covenants, and having been sealed for time and all eternity in the New and Everlasting Order of Matrimony!

"That is how we obtain the Doctoral Degree in Exaltation. Then, and only then, will we be sealed, as families, into our Heavenly Parents' Eternal Family, and be able to go on to have our own Eternal Families."

After a quiet moment of peaceful contemplation, Jehovah arose and, speaking to the group, said, "I am pleased to witness your enduring interest in and continued learning of Our Parent's Plan for our Salvation and Advancement. It pleases Me to see your commitment to the choices and promises you have made here, for in that, I see the hope that you will live with like resolution in the world to which you will be going. And I am pleased to know that you trust and do consult with Orsea. She has gained vast knowledge and freely shares her testimony of all that Father and Mother have taught us."

Then motioning to Orsea to join Him, Jehovah continued with, "Now, there are here among you, others, who too have learned much; I implore you to continue your meeting with them. But now, I must invite Orsea to come with Me; Father and Mother wish to speak with her." As the group watched in thoughtful silence, Jehovah and Orsea stepped down off the Pavilion of Perfection and headed down the Path of Progression toward God's Garden, where Father and Mother were waiting for them.

"Is it time for me to go?" Orsea asked Jehovah.

"Not yet," Jehovah replied, "but that time is not far distant." Then, with an expression of appreciation, He said, "You have prepared yourself well, Orsea; I am pleased."

"Thank you, Jehovah," Orsea said sweetly, "I really appreciate knowing that! It means all the world to me."

Jehovah smiled and asked, with a hint of brotherly fun, "Which world, Orsea, TreLampor or Areth?"

Orsea smiled and replied, with sisterly retort, "Both!"

Then, as they entered the garden, Jehovah said, "You are welcome, Orsea."

And to that, Orsea, again, sweetly replied, "Thank you."

"Orsea," Mother said, stepping up to greet her, "Tell me, how you are feeling?"

"Very happy, Mother, very happy!" Orsea exclaimed.

"That is wonderful," Mother responded, as she sat down with Father and directed Orsea to sit down in front of Them, which she did, right next to Jehovah.

"I know you have been very busy teaching your brothers and sisters," Father said with a grand smile of approval and appreciation. Then asked, "How do you feel they are responding?"

"Well, Father," Orsea began, "first, I want to thank You for permitting me to act as a teacher. I think there is very little that I love to do more than I love to teach."

"We could see that from before the beginning," Father replied with a whimsical smile. "Now," He asked again, "how do you feel they are responding?"

"Well, Father, I am not certain I know exactly how to answer that question," Orsea replied. "Some are responding very well. They seem to understand and accept what they are taught, and honestly desire to know more. They ask a lot of questions because they really do want to understand. They sound like they genuinely want to do what is right when choices are placed before them. But others?"

Orsea paused for a thoughtful moment, then continued with, "Others seem to be more questioning, even challenging. I sometimes feel fear for them, not knowing if I can believe that they really will make the right choices when they are on Areth. They seem... it sounds like... I get the impression that they think they can do things their own way and still get what they want. It troubles me, Father. It saddens me, Mother."

"Yes, Orsea, you see what We see," Mother responded with concern and a bit of sadness in her voice. "That is why We asked Jehovah to invite you to come talk with Us. There are some things that need to be done during the time that you will be on Areth and We want to talk with you about those things because We would like for you to do them.

"Also, some of your brothers and sisters, who will need additional help and attention, will be in the time and places that you will be in. We want to know if you are willing to accept the responsibility of helping them."

"We also have some other assignments for your consideration," Father said. Then He added, "If you are willing to accept the responsibility for them, We will give you some additional instructions related to their possible resolutions. This will require a bit of time, but not more time than you have before it is your time to advance to Areth." Then, with an 'I know there are' expression, Father continued with, "We also want to know if there is anything you would like Us to let you commit yourself to do."

Orsea was silent for a moment. She knew that Their invitation to be Chosen as a Vessel to Serve was quite the compliment! Though she had always put all her uncompromised efforts into learning and sharing Their Plan with everyone, she realized that, like all the others, she still had more to learn, and Areth would be as new an experience for her as it had been or would be for everyone else. She knew she would make mistakes—not deliberate mistakes— but mistakes nonetheless, and she too would have to repent. Still, determined to be as helpful to as many others as she could possibly be, there really was no need for her to contemplate what her answer would be.

"Yes! Yes, of course!" she exclaimed with joy and commitment, "I would love to do anything You would have for me to do, and I do have a few requests of my own."

Jehovah smiled at Orsea, as He teasingly asked, "A few, Orsea? 'Few' is a concept you do not seem to have learned the meaning of. You probably should substitute the identifier, 'a few', with the descriptor, 'a multitude of.'"

"Perhaps You are right, Jehovah," Orsea replied, with a smile and a hint of pride.

In response to the whimsical exchange between Jehovah and Orsea, Father and Mother looked at each other, shook Their heads, and exchanged smiles. After which Father said, "Well then, We should probably get to the planning and training, for there is not a lot of time left before it will be your time to depart."

And that is what They did, that 'moment', and the next 'moment', and the ne... well, you know, for as many 'moments' as were needed. Then, when she was ready, and all things were in place, with sacred enthusiasm, she made her one final request, "May I please go to Areth today? It is a Sabbath Day there! That is the best and most special day of the Areth week, and I want to be there when it starts."

"Yes," Father replied, with a smile. "We knew that would be your preference, so We arranged it."

"And," she added with double the enthusiasm, "can I be there early—Areth early—so that I can be there **in time for church?**"

Mother smiled; she even chuckled a little, wondering if Orsea realized that she would most definitely not be going to church on the day of her arrival on Areth. Nonetheless, to Orsea, She said, "Indeed you may. In fact, We are ready to send you now. You will arrive on the eastern side of Imacera, in Alsynpanveni, at about 3:40 tena irinemad. That is quite early on an Areth morning."

Clasping her hands together, just under her chin, in what would be identified as "prayer mode" on Areth, and with delight, Orsea exclaimed, "Oh, that sounds great!"

Jehovah smiled, shook His head with amused delight, took Orsea's hand, and led her to the Port of Early Departure. Standing on the top step of Heaven's Stairway, He turned Orsea to face Him, then said, "Your best, Orsea, *Right From the Beginning* and always, do your best, continually striving for more, and you will come home."

Orsea smiled and said, with firm commitment and resolve, "I will, Jehovah! I will!!"

Then, Jehovah turned her around to face the stairs, let go of her hand, and whispered sweetly, as she started down the steps, "Go, *Ellie*. Get there... **in time for church!**"

ABOUT THE AUTHOR

Eileen DiStasio-Clark is the second oldest of four children. She is the mother of eleven children and grandmother to twenty-three grandchildren, to date. As a member of The Church of Jesus Christ of Latter-Day Saints, she serves in various positions, teaching, leading, and ministering to children, youth, and adults. Currently, she is also a Family History Missionary. Eileen established the Pursuit of Excellence Institute of Family Education, a non-profit organization focused on strengthening the family. Presently she holds an AA, a BA, and an MA in Clinical Psychology and is working on the completion of her Doctoral Degree.

www.ingramcontent.com/pod-product-compliance
Lightning Source LLC
Chambersburg PA
CBHW042028050526
44107CB00103B/739